I Like Dinosaurs

Angela Aylmore

Heinemann LIBRARY

www.heinemann.co.uk/library
Visit our website to find out more information about Heinemann Library books.

To order:
☎ Phone 44 (0) 1865 888066
   Send a fax to 44 (0) 1865 314091
📄 Visit the Heinemann Bookshop at www.heinemann.co.uk/library to browse our
💻 catalogue and order online.

First published in Great Britain by Heinemann Library, Halley Court, Jordan Hill, Oxford OX2 8EJ, part of Harcourt Education. Heinemann is a registered trademark of Harcourt Education Ltd.

Editorial: Dan Nunn and Sarah Chappelow
Design: Joanna Hinton-Malivoire
Picture research: Erica Newbery
Production: Duncan Gilbert

Origination: Chroma Graphics (Overseas) Pte. Ltd
Printed and bound in China by South China Printing Co. Ltd.

10-digit ISBN 0 431 10953 2
13-digit ISBN 978 0 431 10953 4
11 10 09
10 9 8 7 6 5 4 3

British Library Cataloguing in Publication Data
Aylmore, Angela
   I like dinosaurs. - (Things I like)
   1. Dinosaurs - Juvenile literature
   I. Title
   567.9
A full catalogue record for this book is available from the British Library.

Acknowledgements
The publishers would like to thank the following for permission to reproduce photographs: Alamy pp. **9** (David R. Frazier Photolibrary, Inc.), **20** (Steven May), **21** (Brand X Pictures), **22** (Steven May); NHPA pp. **18–19**.

Illustrations by James Field of Simon Girling and Associates.

Cover photograph of a Tyrannosaurus rex skeleton reproduced with permission of Corbis (Louie Psihoyos).

Contents

Some words are shown in bold, like this. You can find out what they mean by looking in the Glossary.

Dinosaurs

I like dinosaurs. Dinosaurs are animals that lived a very long time ago.

Tyrannosaurus rex

My favourite dinosaur is
Tyrannosaurus rex.

It had very sharp teeth.
These helped it to attack
other dinosaurs!

Tyrannosaurus rex had tiny arms. Each arm had two fingers.

I like to look at Tyrannosaurus rex bones at the **museum**.

Velociraptor

Velociraptor was a small dinosaur. It was even smaller than you!

Scientists think it could run as fast as a car!

Even though Velociraptor was small, it was still dangerous! It had very sharp teeth and claws.

13

Triceratops

This dinosaur is Triceratops.
I think it looks like a rhino!

Triceratops means "horrible three-horned face".

Triceratops ate plants.

Triceratops laid eggs. The eggs **hatched** into baby Triceratops.

Dinosaur fossils

This is a dinosaur **fossil**. Fossils tell us what the dinosaurs looked like.

19

You can see dinosaur fossils
in some **museums**.

Have you ever found a fossil?

Do you like dinosaurs?

Now you know why I like dinosaurs! Do you like dinosaurs too?

Glossary

fossil remains of a plant or animal, usually
found in rocks

hatch to come out of an egg

museum building where people can see
artistic, historic or scientific objects

Find out more

Gone Forever: Tyrannosaurus Rex, Rupert Matthews (Heinemann Library, 2004)

Oxford First Book of Dinosaurs, Barbara Taylor (Oxford University Press, 2003)

Check out this website for more amazing facts:

www.bbc.co.uk/sn/prehistoric_life/

Index

Titles in the *Things I Like* series include:

Hardback   978 0 4311 0960 2

Hardback   978 0 4311 0957 2

Hardback   978 0 4311 0959 6

Hardback   978 0 4311 0953 4

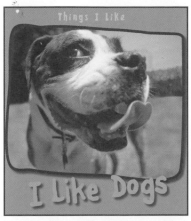

Hardback   978 0 4311 0958 9

Hardback   978 0 4311 0954 1

Hardback   978 0 4311 0956 5

Hardback   978 0 4311 0955 8

Find out about other titles from Heinemann Library on our website www.heinemann.co.uk/library